T0287458

LONDON'S ENVIRO400

DAVID BEDDALL

AMBERLEY

First published 2019

Amberley Publishing
The Hill, Stroud
Gloucestershire, GL5 4EP

www.amberley-books.com

Copyright © David Beddall, 2019

The right of David Beddall to be identified as the Authors of this work has been asserted in accordance with the Copyright, Designs and Patents Act 1988.

ISBN 978 1 4456 8758 2 (print)
ISBN 978 1 4456 8759 9 (ebook)

All rights reserved. No part of this book may be reprinted or reproduced or utilised in any form or by any electronic, mechanical or other means, now known or hereafter invented, including photocopying and recording, or in any information storage or retrieval system, without the permission in writing from the Publishers.

British Library Cataloguing in Publication Data.
A catalogue record for this book is available from the British Library.

Origination by Amberley Publishing.
Printed in the UK.

LONDON'S ENVIRO400

Introduction

The Enviro400 first appeared in 2005 when, in December, the first example was delivered to Stagecoach London. However, it was Metroline that ran the first significant batch of these vehicles on route 24, between Pimlico and Hampstead Heath. In 2006 it replaced the standard Dennis Trident chassis, along with the Alexander ALX400 bodywork, being mainly built as an integral vehicle, although some operators took stock of the chassis on other body styles such as the Optare Olympus. As well as being an integral, the Enviro400 body became a popular choice on the Scania N230UD chassis, mainly with the Stagecoach Group, who put them to use on both town work and the more luxurious Gold networks around the country. The model was also built onto the Volvo B9TL chassis, three of which saw service in London.

A slight remodelling of the bodywork took place and was launched in 2009, featuring small cosmetic changes – mainly with the lights and bumpers. The model continued production until 2015 when it was replaced by the modernised Enviro400 MMC (Major Model Change). The MMC was first introduced in 2014 and coincided with the upgrade to the Euro VI engine specification. The original then became known as the 'classic' model. Like the classic, the MMC became available on the Scania chassis, joined shortly after by the Volvo B5LH model. This latter model was taken up in numbers by various London operators.

A third variant was revealed at the Bus and Coach Expo in October 2015. Named the Enviro400 City, this hybrid model was taken into stock in smaller numbers by London operators, and has seen numerous orders outside London; in particular in Blackpool, Nottingham and Reading. This model took some features from the New Bus for London and the interiors carried by them are the same for each operator.

The classic Enviro400 model totalled over 1,500 examples, both on the diesel and hybrid Enviro400 H model. The Enviro400 MMC model is growing significantly in numbers, the preference being for the integral hybrid version offered by ADL, although the Volvo B5TL and B5LH models also feature in smaller numbers in London fleets. The Enviro400 City model has only been taken up by two London operators so far – Arriva London and CT Plus. All three models feature in this book, which offers a potted history of the type in London service between 2005 and April 2019.

Above and below: Stagecoach London took stock of the first Enviro400 in the capital as a direct replacement for Dennis Trident 17758, destroyed in the 7 July 2005 London terror attack. Originally numbered 18500 (LX55 HGC), this vehicle was adorned with the saying '7 Million Londoners – Spirit of London', a slogan it still carries. It was new in December 2005 and carried a revised livery with a blue skirt. In October 2012, a fire was set on the upper deck causing severe damage to the vehicle. Stagecoach spent a large amount of money on repairs and it re-entered service in April 2013. The re-acquisition of the East London and Selkent businesses in 2011 saw 18500 renumbered 19000. 18500 is shown here attending the London Bus Museums spring gathering, loading in Cobham in original livery, and at Romford Station, after being transferred to Rainham garage in 2015.

Above and below: Under the control of the East London Bus Group, the Selkent division took stock of ten Enviro400s. Stagecoach London won the contract for the 61 between Bromley North and Orpington from First London in 2006, and an order for these vehicles was placed. Delivered over the course of December 2006, these vehicles took up the rolling stock numbers allotted to them by Stagecoach: 19131–19140. In 2010, Stagecoach re-acquired its East London and Selkent operations, with the original Enviro400s slotting into the numbering system as they were intended to. Bromley garage finds 19134 (LX56 EAK) in the new all-red livery adopted by London's operators. Below we see another view of 19134, this time sporting the megasightseeing.com tour livery, introduced by Stagecoach London in 2018. 19131 to 19136 entered service in this guise in April 2019, the remainder of the batch being converted to driver training vehicles. It is seen passing through Mile End, heading for Bow garage.

In a bid to replace the large number of Dennis Tridents operating in East London, Stagecoach placed an order for 124 Enviro400s, for various contract gains. Rainham-based route 174 gained the first examples of this sizeable batch, with 19713–19733 being allocated there. 19713 (LX11 AYU) is seen here loading at Romford Station heading for Dagenham.

Allocated to Plumstead garage for route 99 were fourteen Enviro400s, numbered 19742 to 19755. Like most garages, the vehicles wandered on to other services as required. 19747 (LX11 BCE) demonstrates this, seen operating route 96 (Woolwich–Bluewater). It is seen departing Bluewater Shopping Centre's bus station and bound for Woolwich.

Barking garage took stock of the next batch of Enviro400s to convert a number of services to the type. However, route 62 was not one of them, this being converted years later, with the introduction of the Enviro400 MMC model to Stagecoach. 19756 (LX11 BDF) is seen standing in for one of this type, loading in Barking town centre.

The branding of services passing through the Barkingside area of East London saw several Stagecoach vehicles gain route branding. 19776 (LX11 BFV) is showing off its branding for route 169, whilst negotiating Ilford Broadway, destined for Clayhall on route 169. 19776 was new to Barking garage in April 2011.

19812 (LX11 BKD) was originally allocated to Plumstead garage to operate the 53 (Plumstead Garage–Whitehall, Horse Guards). The intake of new Enviro400 MMC hybrids in 2016 saw a number of these vehicles reallocated around Stagecoach London. 19812 moved north to North Street, Romford garage. It is seen approaching Romford Station whilst operating route 496 to the local hospital.

A sunny Woolwich finds 19823 (LX11 BKY) heading towards Orpington Station on route 51. This was another example new to Plumstead garage for route 53.

Stagecoach received its first batch of hybrid Enviro400s in the opening months of 2012. Twenty-six were initially taken into stock to replace the older Alexander ALX400 bodied Dennis Tridents operating route 15 (Blackwall–Oxford Circus). The route lost its Enviro400s from the beginning of March 2015 when it was converted to the New Bus for London. The examples from the 15 transferred across to Leyton garage where they were put to use on route 56. It is on this route we find 12142 (LX61 DDV) passing Hackney Downs Station wearing an advertisement for London Metropolitan University.

12149 (LX61 DCU) is seen here on its intended route 15 at Trafalgar Square. This photograph allows you to make comparisons between the front stylings of the Plaxton President and Enviro400 models.

19852 (LX12 CZF) was new to Stagecoach London in March 2012 to help update a number of services operating into Stratford. It is seen here operating route 104, having just reached journeys end at Stratford Bus Station.

Seen at the same location is 19866 (LX12 CZV). It was one of a number of Enviro400s allocated to West Ham garage in April 2012. It is seen operating route 238, having travelled into Stratford from Barking.

West Ham garage took stock of twelve Enviro400s to take up service on route 238 (Stratford–Barking) in April 2012. Seen entering Stratford Bus Station is 10101 (LX12 DAU). Nationally, the Stagecoach Group took stock of a large volume of Enviro400s between 2006 and 2012. This resulted in the company running out of numbers in the 19000 series that was initially allocated to the type. New diesel examples were, as demonstrated here, placed into the new numbering sequence of 10000s.

March 2019 saw the transfer of route 20 from Go-Ahead London to CT Plus. A delay in the reduction of PVR on route 388 led to a shortfall of vehicles required to operate the route, as it was intended that the surplus vehicles from the 388 would transfer to route 20. To compensate this, Stagecoach London loaned 10113 and 10114 to CT Plus for a short while. 10113 (LX12 DCZ) is seen departing Walthamstow Bus Station on the first day of operation of route 20 by its new company. CT Plus Walthamstow Stadium garage codes (AW) were applied to these vehicles, as can be seen in this photograph.

May 2012 saw Leyton garage receive 10113 to 10123 for the take up of service 275 (Barkingside Tesco–St James Street Station). The contract renewed in March, and since the Enviro400s were late in arriving, the faithful Alexander ALX400 bodied Dennis Trident stood in for the late comers. In 2017, branding was applied to buses operating through the Barkingside area of East London as an experiment. Route numbers on bus stops were coloured to match the colour of branding applied to the vehicles. The 275 was one such route to gain this branding, as seen here applied to 10115 (LX12 DDE). It represents the batch and is seen departing Walthamstow Central Bus Station.

Transport for London dubbed 2014 the 'Year of the Bus', with various events taking place to celebrate London's buses. A handful of vehicles also received commemorative liveries to help celebrate. One such example was Stagecoach London 10136 (LX12 DFN). It gained the livery worn by Woolwich Corporation Tramways. It is seen here in April 2014 attending the spring gathering at the Brooklands Museum in Surrey.

10155 (EU62 AXT) was delivered to North Street, Romford, in September 2012, for use on route 175. It later transferred to Leyton garage for use on services from there. It is seen exiting Walthamstow Bus Station sporting an advertisement for the Oyster off-peak ticket applied to the vehicle in February 2019.

The award of routes 103 and 175, the latter from First London to Stagecoach required the company to purchase some new vehicles for them. Nine such vehicles were received by North Street, Romford garage in September and November 2012 for these routes. This small batch unusually received Essex registration marks as shown here by EU62 AZA, which took up rolling stock number 10159 with the company. It is seen about to pass Romford Station heading towards Collier Row. An Enviro400 MMC can be glimpsed in the background.

A year passed before the arrival of any more diesel Enviro400s with Stagecoach. The company was successful in winning several tenders from First London, leading to the demise of this company. 10165 (SN63 JVO) was ordered against the tender wins on the 252 and 365 in the Romford area. 10165 to 10171 were allocated to Rainham garage. They were also put to use on other double-deck routes, as can be seen here. Romford Station is the location of this photograph.

Route 179 (Barking–Chingford) was the other service won by Stagecoach London from First in 2013. Leyton garage were allocated 10172–10193 to operate this service. However, 10172 (SN63 JVX) is another example seen off its intended route. This time it is heading to St James Street, exiting Walthamstow Central Bus Station.

The Stagecoach Group operate the low-cost coaching unit megabus.com, linking many UK destinations. 10182 (SN63 JWK) gained an advertisement for this operation in March 2014, and is seen showing it off whilst on layover at Chingford Station.

Sixty-three Enviro400H hybrids were ordered by Stagecoach for 2014 delivery, awarded against a number of tender wins, mostly in South East London. Two routes of interest were the 54 (Woolwich–Lewisham) and 75 (Lewisham–Croydon) which took thirty-two examples, all being allocated to Catford garage. 12292 (SN14 TXL), the last example, represents this batch, seen reaching journey's end at Woolwich.

Eleven E40Hs were allocated to Plumstead garage, bridging the gap between those at Catford (12261–12292) and Bow (12304–12333). 12297 (SN14 TXS) was decorated in the Poppy Appeal livery and is seen in Woolwich having completed a journey on route 53 from Whitehall.

2014 saw over 100 hybrid Enviro400s taken into stock by Stagecoach London for various routes in both North East and South East London. Bow garage took stock of thirty-one examples for use on route 205 (Paddington–Bow Church), on which they replaced Scania Omnicity double-decks. 12330 (SL14 LNW) is seen passing through Mile End heading towards Paddington.

Stagecoach London won the contract for route 498 from Go-Ahead London in 2015 for which it ordered seven Enviro400 MMCs. The batch were slightly late in being delivered so the route was initially operated by Dennis Tridents. Romford Station finds 10303 (YY15 OYU) heading for Brentwood.

Stagecoach London added twenty-one Enviro400 MMC bodied Volvo B5LHs to its Plumstead allocation over the summer of 2015 to operate route 177, between Thamesmead and Peckham. 13080 (BF15 KGO) is seen passing the *Cutty Sark* at Greenwich bound for Thamesmead.

Twenty-one further examples of the Volvo B5LH/Enviro400 MMC combination were taken into stock by Stagecoach London in December 2015 and January 2016. Allocated to Catford garage, these vehicles took up service on route 47 between Shoreditch and Bellingham, Catford bus garage. 13101 (BL65 OYX) is seen heading to the latter destination, passing through Lewisham town centre.

Stagecoach ordered forty additional Enviro400 MMCs to convert routes 62 and 294 to the type, along with top ups for routes 145, 174 and 496. 10313 (SN16 OJT) arrived with the company in March 2016 and is seen on layover in Ilford.

May 2017 saw Barking-based 10324 (SN16 OKF) decorated in a lime green livery for World Environment Day in June 2017. It is captured sporting this in Ilford.

10325 (SN16 OKG) represents the batch of Enviro400 MMCs that converted route 62 from Optare Versa operation to double-decks. It is seen shortly after delivery passing through Barking town centre.

June and July 2016 saw the delivery of thirty-six AD E40H MMCs to Plumstead garage to primarily convert route 53 (Whitehall, Horse Guards–Plumstead Station) to the type. The arrival of these vehicles allowed the diesel Enviro400s based at Plumstead to be cascaded within Stagecoach London to replace other, older types. 12367 (YX16 OGF) is seen heading towards Whitehall at Woolwich town centre.

Stagecoach London received twenty-three E40Hs at Bow garage in January and February 2017 primarily for route 277, although a number strayed onto route 205. 12419 (YY66 PKC) is seen just leaving the stop for Dalston Junction Overground Station bound for nearby Highbury Corner.

After leaving the Dalston Junction area, route 277 makes progress towards Crossharbour, travelling through a range of East London locations including Mile End. 12424 (YY66 PXU) is seen crossing the busy intersection linking central London with Stratford and Ilford.

A more modest batch of seven Enviro400 MMCs arrived in September 2017 to take up service on the 257 from Leyton garage. These vehicles were supported by other buses from the Leyton allocation to make up the numbers needed. 12429 (YX67 VBF) is seen here entering Stratford Bus Station shortly after arrival in the capital.

Plumstead garage took stock of nineteen further AD E40Hs for the takeover of route 161 from Metrobus in February 2018, well ahead of the takeover of the service in March. 12443 (SN67 XEH) is one example of the batch seen passing through Woolwich en route for North Greenwich.

The summer of 2018 saw the arrival of sixty-three Smart Hybrid Enviro400 MMCs with Stagecoach London, the first of their type. The initial plan was to allocate them all to West Ham garage and concentrate them on services in North East London primarily on those serving Canning Town. However, a small batch were diverted to SelKent for use from Catford garage. 11035 (SN18 KUB) is seen on route 330 at Canning Town Bus Station. A number of these vehicles were fitted with white electric blinds, as shown here; however, they were not easy to capture on camera.

Metroline was the first London company to place orders for the Enviro400, with twenty-eight examples being ordered for route 24 (Pimlico–Hampstead Heath). The company had introduced a new, single numbering sequence by the time the vehicles were taken into stock, therefore the batch was numbered TE665–692. These, along with a batch of ADL Darts delivered at the same time, were the only vehicles in the fleet to be delivered with a pastel blue skirt. TE670 (LK55 KKB) shows off this livery whilst travelling through Piccadilly Circus towards Hampstead Heath. The curvature of Regent Street can be seen to the right of the photograph. (David Beddall)

From the same batch is TE674 (LK55 KKF). It is seen paused on London Bridge, dwarfed by the skyscrapers in the background. It is seen nearing journey's end on route 17, operated from Holloway garage.

December 2010 saw heavy snowfall in London, as is depicted above. TE683 (LK55 KKS) is seen negotiating Aldwych whilst operating route 91 to Trafalgar Square. Apart from the registration, the vehicle and route are almost unidentifiable. (David Beddall)

New to Holloway garage for route 134, TE712–723 were the next deliveries of the Enviro400 to Metroline, reverting back to the darker blue skirt. They later migrated across to Edgware garage. TE720 (LK56 FHP) is seen exiting Brent Cross Bus Station bound for Northwick Park Hospital.

Brent Cross also finds TE722 (LK56 FHS). It is seen on layover before operating another journey on route 186. Brent Cross is also served by a number of single-deck routes as can be seen in this photograph.

Twenty Enviro400s were ordered against the award of new route 332 at Cricklewood garage, which were numbered TE828–847. Delivery took place over the course of September 2007 in time for the route to start in October. However, many of the Enviro400s were put to use on route 16 between Cricklewood and Victoria. The latter location is where we find TE830 (LK57 AXH), just starting its journey north.

Seen stopped opposite the new Cricklewood bus garage is TE882 (LK08 DXU). This was one of forty-two Enviro400s ordered for 2008 delivery against routes 460 and E2. They were reallocated to Cricklewood where they were used on the 16, along with hybrid examples for comparison of the two types. However, the batch, as can be seen in this photograph, strayed from the 16. TE882 is seen operating a journey on route 332 towards Paddington Station.

TE892 (LK08 NVG) is another Enviro400 new to Cricklewood garage for route 16. It is seen when operating from Perivale garage on route 297. Ealing Broadway provides the backdrop to this photograph. (David Beddall)

As is typical with many London operators, the influx of new buses for central area routes sees the cascade of slightly older vehicles out to the edges of the capital. TE898 (LK08 NVO) shows this rather well. Originally delivered to Cricklewood garage in August 2008, this vehicle later transferred to Potters Bar garage. It is seen here in Barnet operating route 263 to Highbury Barn.

Originally allocated to Cricklewood, the conversion of route 263 in 2009 saw the transfer of TE909–914 to Holloway. TE910 (LK58 COH) is seen here going the wrong way around Aldwych before crossing the River Thames to terminate at nearby Waterloo. The road closure was implemented by the annual Lord Mayor's Parade, which closes streets in the City of London and parts of central London.

Slotted in amongst the standard diesel Enviro400s were five hybrid Enviro400 Hs. They displaced TE909–914 to Holloway garage. TE910 is seen in the previous photograph. TEH915 was registered by Alexander Dennis themselves, sporting a Scottish registration mark (SN08 AAO). All but TEH915 entered service on the 16 from Cricklewood in December 2008, the vehicle above joining them in January 2009. TEH915 is seen above showing off the green leaf livery applied to the initial batch of hybrid vehicles in London whilst parked at Cricklewood garage. (David Beddall)

Archway Station is a hub for Metroline services, with the majority operating from nearby Holloway garage. However, route 263 (Holloway–Barnet Hospital) is operated by a batch of Enviro400s from Potters Bar garage. TE936 (LK09 EXR) is seen passing through Archway bound for Barnet Hospital.

Another example of the 263 batch is TE941 (LK58 KHF). It is seen having a day out on route 217 (Waltham Cross–Turnpike Lane). It is seen on layover at the Turnpike Lane Station terminus showing the full Metroline livery in its glory.

The closing three months of 2010 saw a number of Enviro400s, both diesel and hybrid, delivered to Cricklewood garage to convert routes 139, 189 and 210 to the type. TE1087 (LK60 AFY) was one of thirty-two diesel examples delivered to the garage at this time. It is seen operating a journey on route 32, about to enter Edgware Bus Station. A comparison of the Enviro400 and ALX400 models can be made in this photograph.

TE1103 (LK60 AHP) is seen on one of its intended routes, the 189. In November 2011, it gained an all-over advertisement (minus the front), for the Christmas period at the newly opened M&M store in Leicester Square. It is seen on layover at Marble Arch.

TEH1105–1114 completed the conversion of routes 139, 189 and 210 to Enviro400. TEH1113 (LK60 AJY) is seen travelling down Oxford Street heading towards West Hampstead. By the introduction of this batch into London service, the advertisement of the vehicle as a hybrid was somewhat toned down when compared to that applied to TEH915 shown earlier in the book.

Twenty-six hybrid Enviro400s were delivered to Metroline in the autumn months of 2011 to help convert routes 16, 139 and 189 fully to type. TEH1220 (LK61 BJX) is seen heading to Waterloo, travelling down Haymarket, having just negotiated Piccadilly Circus. (David Beddall)

Eleven Enviro400s were delivered to Metroline in May 2012 for the intended use on route 32 from Cricklewood. They were placed into store and used on Olympic duties in July and August 2012. One rule regarding the use of buses on Olympic contracts was that they were not allowed to carry fleet names. This can be clearly seen here in this view of TE1312 (LK12 AWA), which is seen exiting the Eaton Manor Transport Hub, with an array of other buses from operators around the UK seen in the background.

Twenty-eight diesel Enviro400s were allocated to Potters Bar garage to operate service 82. However, these vehicles did not always stay true to this route, venturing out on other double-deck services from Potters Bar. TE1426 (LK62 DYA) shows this practice, being captured travelling through Holloway on route 263 towards Barnet Hospital.

Potters Bar garage took control of route 134 in the spring of 2019 from Holloway. To fill in the gaps in delivery of new VMH-class MCV EvoSetis, a number of Enviro400s were initially used on the service. TE1434 (LK13 BEU) is seen entering Tottenham Court Road heading towards North Finchley. The bottom of Centre Point can be seen on the right of this photograph.

Twenty-one Enviro400s were ordered against the retention of route 82 (Victoria–North Finchley) in 2013. Delivery of the batch took place in February and March 2013 to Potters Bar garage. TE1437 (LK13 BFF) is seen here passing through Barnet off route on the 307, heading towards Barnet Hospital.

TE1441 (LK13 BFN) is seen on its intended route 82, parked at the North Finchley terminus of the service. In 2017 the 82 was withdrawn and replaced by a re-routed 13, which passed to Tower Transit.

Nineteen E400Hs arrived at Cricklewood in March and April 2013 to finish the conversion of route 189 to the type. This allowed the cascade of older diesel Enviro400s to Edgware garage, converting the garage's double-deck allocation fully to this type. TEH1452 (LK13 BGU) is seen about to pass through Trafalgar Square shortly after delivery.

The TEHs were often found operating other double-deck routes out of Cricklewood garage, as demonstrated by TEH1456 (LK13 BGZ). It is seen about to leave Kilburn High Road to complete its journey to nearby Kilburn Park.

Seen out of its normal operating area is TEH1458 (LK13 BHD). It is seen about to cross Putney Bridge, operating as a rail replacement service for the District Line.

On 22 June 2013, Metroline acquired part of the First London Empire, with garages at Willesden Junction, Hayes, Uxbridge and Greenford, transferring all vehicles allocated to these garages. A number of Enviro400s were included in the sale, and were slotted into the Metroline fleet numbering sequence. Twelve examples allocated to Uxbridge took up rolling stock numbers TE1571–1582 and were used on the express service 607 between White City and Uxbridge. TE1580 (LK08 FNA) is seen offloading passengers at Shepherds Bush Station.

TE1745 (SN09 CGE) formed part of a larger batch of vehicles (TE1715–1751) allocated to Greenford garage where they were originally used on local services E1 and E3. The loss of these services to other operators led to the cascade of many examples of this batch to other Metroline garages to replace older vehicles. TE1745 is seen here operating from Uxbridge garage, passing through Shepherds Bush Green, bound for nearby White City.

A small contingent of the new MMC model were taken into stock by Metroline in the spring of 2015, with sixteen examples in total entering the fleet. These were to be the only examples of the type to be purchased by Metroline. Unlike other operators, Metroline insisted on registering these vehicles themselves, giving them London registration marks rather than Scottish or Yorkshire marks, as had become typical with other operators. TEH2087 (LK15 CSU) is seen operating route 332, their intended route, passing through Kilburn.

Above and below: The Enviro400 MMC TEH-class commonly strayed on to the 139 before the route passed to London Sovereign. Demonstrating this is TEH2080 (LK15 CSY) at Waterloo and TEH2083 (LK15 CTF) at a wet Aldwych.

E1 (SN06 BNA) was one of fifteen Enviro400s initially ordered by the Go-Ahead London group to operate route 196 from Stockwell garage. E1 put in an appearance in April 2006. November 2007 saw the addition of route 24 to Stockwell, leading to the 196 batch being mixed with the 24 batch. This is seen here with E1 captured travelling up Whitehall towards Hampstead Heath. (David Beddall)

The original batch of Enviro400s for the 196 turned twelve years old in 2018. During the year they were taken out of mainstream London service and added to the commercial service fleet to update it. E3 (SN06 BNB) is seen in its new guise at St Pancras International Station complete with its new electronic blind.

Peckham garage gained an allocation of twenty-one Enviro400s in May and June 2006 for route 37 (Peckham–Clapham Junction). E33 (LX06 EZH) is seen starting its journey out to Peckham whilst negotiating the crossroads at Clapham Junction.

2012 saw a number of Enviro400s with Go-Ahead London gain all-over advertisements for Vodafone. E40 (LX56 ETD) is seen showing off this livery and is about to enter Bexleyheath town centre before starting a journey on route 486 to North Greenwich. E40 formed part of a batch of seventeen Enviro400s delivered to Bexleyheath garage in 2007 to convert the 486 to double-deck operation.

Seventeen Enviro400s were ordered for the London Central operation in August 2006 to convert route 486 (Bexleyheath–North Greenwich) from single to double-deck. The first examples began to arrive in January 2007, all being delivered by February. Bexleyheath finds E56 (LX56 EUD) on layover before returning to North Greenwich Station. The London Central fleet names can be clearly seen in this view. (David Beddall)

E67 (LX57 CJJ) is another example of the batch originally allocated to Stockwell for route 24. The batch was later split and transferred around the Go-Ahead London group as required. E67 made it to the reaches of Bexleyheath. Route 89 gained its own allocation of Enviro400s in 2012. This batch stood out from others initially as they carried the London General fleet names instead of London Central ones as can be seen above.

Whitehall finds E86 (LX57 CKV), another one of the 24 batch, complete with London General fleet names. Bound for Pimlico, Horse Guards Parade provides the background to this photograph.

London Central's New Cross garage gained six Enviro400s to help out on route 36, all arriving with the company in April 2008. The first of the batch, E94 (LX08 EBP), is seen here at Vauxhall Bus Station. (David Beddall)

The original hybrid vehicles that entered service in London carried green-leaf livery, making them stand out from the conventional London bus. Five Enviro400H models were introduced to the Go-Ahead London fleet during the latter part of 2008. Representing this batch is EH1 (LX58 DDJ) seen in full green-leaf livery having just passed Victoria Station. The original five later gained repaints into the more subtle hybrid livery.

Go-Ahead London took stock of a trio of ADL Enviro400 bodied Volvo B9TLs in 2008. VE1–3 were allocated to the company's Putney garage, from where they were initially put to use on route 85. Above we see VE3 (LX58 CWM) passing through Kingston on the Sutton-based route 213. These three vehicles remained the only examples of this combination to operate in the UK.

Go-Ahead London won the contract for route 57 (Clapham Park–Kingston) from London United in July 2016 when displaced Enviro400s from other services were put to use on the route. E126 (LX09 FCC) was one such vehicle and is seen passing Cromwell Road Bus Station, Kingston, setting out on its journey to Clapham Junction.

October 2010 saw the arrival of nine Enviro400s at Stockwell to partly renew the rolling stock on route 88. E135 (SN60 BZG) is seen heading towards Clapham Common whilst circumnavigating Trafalgar Square. The base of Nelson's Column can be seen towering above the bus.

2017 saw Go-Ahead London gain route 5 (Canning Town–Romford Market) from Stagecoach London. E137 (SN60 BZJ) is seen passing through Plaistow bound for Romford Market.

E156 (SN11 BUH) is seen standing at a rainy Richmond Bus Station. Go-Ahead London took over route 337 from the Original London Sightseeing Tour in 2011. The batch E151–162 were additional examples allocated to Stockwell garage.

Route 453 lost its bendy buses during September 2011 in favour of a large number of Enviro400s. E192 (SN61 BJU) represents the batch here, heading towards Deptford Bridge at Piccadilly Circus. This vehicle shows off the new Go-Ahead London fleet names, with the operating company displayed in white underneath this.

The Denmark Hill stop in Camberwell finds E200 (SN61 BKF). This was another example originally purchased for the conversion of route 453 to the type. It is seen heading towards Dulwich Library on route 40.

The introduction of new vehicles into the Go-Ahead London fleet saw the reallocation of a number of Enviro400s around the company. E210 (SN61 DDE) was transferred across to the Metrobus operation and is seen here at Bromley South operating a journey on route 320 to Catford Bridge.

The Northumberland Park operation of First London passed to Go-Ahead London control in March 2012. The fleet was differentiated from the original Go-Ahead London fleet by the addition of the letter 'N' to the fleet number. Showing this is EN17 (SN58 CFJ), which is seen departing Turnpike Lane on route 231 towards Enfield Chase.

Fifteen Enviro400s arrived in June 2012 and were placed into store, minus any fleet names. A month later they were put to use on contract work for the London 2012 Olympic Games. E246 (YX12 FPA) is seen here exiting the Eaton Manor Transport set up opposite the Olympic Village. For extra security measures, any panels that could be opened were sealed using blue tape as can be seen when looking around the light area.

An increase in the PVR on route 231 in 2013 required an extra vehicle. This was fulfilled by the arrival of E276 (SN13 CJE). E276 was originally destined for Merton, with E280 being the example to be allocated to Northumberland Park garage for the 231. However, blinds for the latter garage were fitted to E276 at the factory and therefore it was allocated to Northumberland Park in place of E280. It is seen here at Turnpike Lane.

The first single-doored Enviro400s for London arrived in 2014 and were placed into the Go-Ahead London commercial fleet, with three examples arriving in March. E281 (YX14 RTV) was allocated to New Cross garage and gained the grey-skirt livery that had become synonymous with Go-Ahead London. It is seen here at Brooklands Museum attending the 2013 spring gathering.

Go-Ahead London took stock of sixteen AD Enviro400 MMC bodied Volvo B5LHs in June 2015 to take up service on route 135 (Old Street Station–Crossharbour). EHV15 (BL15 HCD) is seen stopped outside Liverpool Street Station heading towards Old Street.

Go-Ahead London won the contracts for routes 35 and 40 from Abellio London, starting in April 2016. For this, twenty-two Enviro400 MMCs were ordered, alongside a number of MCV EvoSeti-bodied Volvo B5TLs. EH48 (YX16 OCD) is seen loading at the Denmark Hill stop in Camberwell bound for Clapham Junction.

Route 363 was next to receive the new model in 2016. Thirteen MMCs arrived during October and November, and is represented here by EH61 (YX66 WHC). It is seen loading in Peckham town centre, heading for Elephant & Castle.

The winter of 2016/17 saw the delivery of thirty-nine Enviro400 MMCs to Go-Ahead London's Putney garage, to help improve the air quality of Putney High Street itself. These vehicles were joined by a large number of Wright Eclipse Gemini 3 bodied Volvo B5LHs for other routes from Putney. The original order was for a similar number of Volvo B5LH vehicles with the Enviro400 MMC body style. The first of the batch, EH74 (YY66 OYB), is seen about to cross Putney Bridge, having just travelled in from Baker Street on route 74.

EH79 (YY66 OYH) became the first Enviro400 MMC in London to gain an all-over advertisement for the 2018 Winter Olympics in South Korea. It is seen rounding Hyde Park Corner showing off this livery, whilst heading toward Putney Heath on route 14.

February 2017 saw the arrival of a pair of Enviro400 MMCs with Go-Ahead London for the Commercial Services fleet. These varied from other examples delivered to the company in that they were built to single-door layout. The grey-skirt livery also made a comeback on these two vehicles, along with gold fleet names. E285 (SN66 WNF) is seen at St Pancras having just operated a journey from Wimbledon.

Eighteen further examples (EH113–130) were ordered against the tender win on route 42, converting the route to double-deck operation. This batch formed a common user pool of vehicles, alongside the MCV EvoSetis, and were used as required on routes 35, 40, 42 and 185 from Camberwell. EH115 (SN66 WOA) is seen demonstrating this when captured crossing London Bridge, bound for Clapham Junction.

EH133 (YW17 JTY) was one of thirty-one Enviro400 MMCs delivered to Go-Ahead London's Blue Triangle division to fully convert route 115 (Aldgate–East Ham) and partially convert route 5 (Canning Town–Romford Market) upon takeover from Stagecoach. Canning Town provides the backdrop for this photograph, with the Docklands Light Railway Station visible in the background. The 5 is interworked with Volvo B9TLs that had previously worked on the East London Transit network.

From the same batch comes EH142 (YW17 JUO). It is seen on its first day of service on route 115, passing the end of the East Ham town centre, shortly before terminating at Central Park. Newnham Town Hall is located just behind the camera.

October 2017 saw the arrival of nine Enviro400 MMCs for the partial conversion of route 176 when it was taken over from Arriva London. EH166 (YX67 VFL) is seen loading in Waterloo bound for Tottenham Court Road.

EH211 (YY67 UTL) was part of a batch of ninety-three Enviro400 MMCs taken into stock in early 2018 to convert routes 36, 172, 343 and X68 to the type. EH211 is found negotiating Elephant & Castle whilst heading towards Clerkenwell Green on route 172.

Merton garage took stock of twenty-six Enviro400 MMCs in June 2018, to convert route 77 to the type. It was joined by twenty-one other examples to partially convert routes 87 and 171 to the Enviro400 MMC. EH296 (YX18 KXJ) is seen here passing through Tooting Broadway before shortly arriving at journeys end at Tooting Station.

LJ56 VTK was one of twenty-seven such examples to enter service with Travel London in January 2007 to operate the newly created route 452 (Kensal Rise–Wandsworth Road Station). The batch was late arriving, being covered for by Alexander ALX400 bodied Dennis Tridents until the full compliment arrived. This vehicle was originally numbered ED8, later becoming 9408. In June 2009 it passed to Abellio London who it is seen operating route 452 for. Notting Hill Gate provides the backdrop in this photograph.

Seen on layover at Aldgate Bus Station is 9438 (LJ09 CBX), running with its original operator, Travel London. The company was successful in winning the tender for routes 35 (Clapham Junction–Shoreditch) and 40 (Aldgate–Dulwich Library) in September 2008. Along with the contract renewal on route 156 (Vauxhall–Wimbledon), Travel London placed an order for fifty-seven Enviro400s for the three services. 9438 was allocated to Walworth garage for use on route 40. (David Beddall)

Route 414 travels from Maida Hill to Putney Bridge Station, passing through Marble Arch and Hyde Park Corner. The route terminates just before crossing Putney Bridge itself. All Saints Church, Fulham, dominates the background of this photograph of 9509 (SN59 AVW) at Putney Bridge Station. This vehicle was one of nineteen such examples that entered service in November 2009 from Battersea garage on the 414.

Another example of the 414 batch was captured heading back towards Putney Bridge, having just worked a short journey to Marble Arch. It is at this busy location we find 9522 (SN59 AWR) – the penultimate example of the nineteen Enviro400s purchased for use on the 414.

An order for thirteen hybrid Enviro400H vehicles was placed in the spring of 2011 for the partial conversion of route 188 (Russell Square–North Greenwich). Delivery commenced in December that year, the vehicles entered service on the route alongside the Wright Eclipse Gemini bodied Volvo B7TL machines already on the service. 2404 (SN61 DFU) was one of the December deliveries. It is seen here at Canada Water Bus Station heading to Peckham on route 381.

2012 saw a large number of both diesel and hybrid versions of the Enviro400 taken into stock by Abellio London. 9551 (SN12 AOY) was taken into stock by Abellio London in May 2012 and allocated to Battersea garage. Canada Water Bus Station again provides the backdrop for this photograph, where 9551 is seen exiting before heading towards North Greenwich Station.

A third photograph taken at Canada Water is of Abellio London's 9553 (SN12 APF). In recent years it has become more popular to place advertisements on London's buses. 9553 carried a purple-based livery for Zoopla between September 2016 and April 2017.

Abellio won the contract for route E1 between Greenford and Ealing Broadway. For this, a small batch of Enviro400s were delivered to Hayes garage. 2447 (SK14 CUG) is seen departing Greenford Broadway destined for Ealing Broadway.

A wet Ealing Broadway finds 2450 (SK14 SYZ), which has just completed its journey from Greenford Broadway. The E1 rounds the scenic green opposite Ealing Broadway Station before heading back towards Greenford.

A larger batch of twenty-two Enviro400s arrived with Abellio London during July and August 2014 when route 49 (White City–Clapham Junction) was acquired from London United. Whilst 2465–2486 were the batch allocated to this service, other examples from the Battersea allocation could be found operating the service. This is demonstrated by 2452 (SL14 DDF), which is seen almost at journey's end at Shepherds Bush Station. 2452 formed part of a batch taken into stock to operate route C3.

Another example to demonstrate a common user pool attitude at Battersea garage is seen here. 2469 (SN64 OET) formed part of the batch intended to operate route 49, but is seen travelling down Park Lane on route 414 (Putney Bridge–Maida Hill) – a service normally operated by diesel Enviro400s.

Abellio London won the contract for route 49 from London United to start in September 2014. For this, twenty-one Enviro400 hybrids were taken into stock, the majority over the course of July and August for the take up of the route. 2476 (SN64 OFA) is seen here, having just dropped off passengers at Shepherds Bush Underground Station prior to passing the White City Westfield Shopping Centre.

Abellio London placed the first order for the Enviro400 MMC, by a London operator, in 2014, when the company won the tenders for routes 109 and 415 in South London. Forty-five examples were initially ordered by the company for these two routes, and the lone double-deck working on route 407, 2507 (YY64 TZG), is seen here in Croydon.

YY64 GXG, 2400, made its London debut in 2014 at the Walworth garage open day, albeit un-registered at this time. It is seen here in this view passing through Brixton town centre. This prototype Enviro400 MMC entered service with Abellio London in December 2014, operating twice for this company before returning to Alexander Dennis in May 2017. It now operates with Uno Buses in Northampton.

Walworth garage finds 2519 (YX15 OWH), with 2516 (YX15 OWE) visible to the right. Walworth is home to the allocation of 109 and 415 vehicles. An example of the classic Enviro400 can just be glimpsed behind 2519.

Abellio London took stock of eighteen Enviro400 MMCs in August 2016 to operate route 344 from Hayes garage. 2535 (YY16 YKB) is seen approaching Clapham Junction shortly after arrival with the company.

May 2018 saw Abellio London take over route 196 from Go-Ahead London, for which sixteen Enviro400 MMCs were taken into stock. 2608 (SN18 KKX) is seen straying off route, heading to Kings Cross on route 45, passing through Elephant & Castle.

Above and below: November 2017 saw the transfer of route 45 from Go-Ahead London to Abellio London with the introduction of yet more Enviro400 MMCs to the company. Here we see 2580 (YY67 GZA) and 2601 (YY67 GZX), both in the St Pancras area. 2580 is seen about to enter Euston Road, whilst 2601 is seen parked outside the main rail terminal.

July 2017 saw the renumbering of the Quality Line fleet into the main RATP Group numbering sequence. Originally numbered DD04, SK07 DZD took up new fleet number ADE40296 at this time. It is seen about to embark on its journey to Epsom, waiting to depart Cromwell Road Bus Station, Kingston.

Quality Line won its first double-deck route contracts in October 2006 for the 406 and 418, both travelling different ways between Kingston and Epsom. For this, an initial order for ten Enviro400s was placed to cover both routes. The last of the batch, DD10 (SK07 DZL), arrived with the company during June 2007. It is seen here on layover at Cromwell Road Bus Station, Kingston.

The London Bus Museum takes over the Brooklands Museum site for its annual spring bus rally. This is where we find DD17 (SL14 LNG) entering the site. DD17 was one of five Enviro400s taken into stock to cover a significant increase in the peak vehicle requirement (PVR) on route 418.

DN33502 (LK57 EJO) was delivered to First London in December 2007 and allocated to First Capital's Dagenham garage. They were purchased to operate route 498 but a delay in the start of the contract saw 33501 and 33502 put to use on the ELW contract, alongside some redundant Plaxton Presidents. They were eventually returned to the correct route, before becoming part of the common user pool of vehicles at Dagenham. DN33502 is seen at Chingford Station, having operated a journey on the 179 from Ilford. The route was later lost to Stagecoach. (David Beddall)

DN33514 (LK08 FMX) was one of eleven vehicles originally allocated to Westbourne Park for use on route 23 (Westbourne Park–Liverpool Street Station). The introduction of newer vehicles on the route saw the original Enviro400s cascaded out to Uxbridge where they were predominantly used on the 607 between Uxbridge and White City. It is seen stopped at Shepherds Bush Station. They later passed to Metroline along with Uxbridge garage. (David Beddall)

June 2008 saw the conversion of route 231 (Turnpike Lane–Enfield Chase) to the Enviro400, with Northumberland Park garage receiving an allocation of six examples. DN33526 (LK08 FLR) was numerically the last of the six for this route. It is seen on layover at Turnpike Lane Station shortly after arrival. (David Beddall)

Turnpike Lane Station also finds DN33537 (SN58 CEY). Seventeen examples, DN33527–33543, were allocated to Northumberland Park garage and were shared between routes 191 (Brimsdown–Lower Edmonton) and the 231. All examples allocated to Northumberland Park transferred to Go-Ahead London in March 2012. (David Beddall)

Dagenham garage received a large quantity of Enviro400s for routes 179, 252 and 365 between October and December 2008. DN33556 (SN58 CGG) was one such example to arrive over this period. This was the first batch to receive white First logos. It is seen parked at Chingford Station waiting to start a journey back to Ilford.

DN33563 (SN58 CGZ) is another example of the Dagenham batch. It is seen heading towards Mardyke Estate on route 365, passing Romford Station. A comparison between the Enviro400 and ALX400 models can be made.

Thirty-seven Enviro400s were taken into stock at Greenford garage during 2009 to replace older Plaxton Presidents on routes E1 and E3. DN33587 (SN09 CEX) represents the batch and is seen here parked at Greenford Broadway. The E1 travels between Greenford Broadway and Ealing Broadway. (David Beddall)

25 June 2011 saw First London place almost 100 new buses into service from Lea Interchange garage across three routes – the 25, 26 and 30. The latter two routes saw the introduction of forty-four Enviro400s on this date. It wasn't long before they were used on different routes operated from Lea Interchange. Two years later the batch transferred across to the Tower Transit operations. This is with whom we see DN33615 (SN11 BMZ) operating with. It is seen operating route 425 at journeys end at Stratford Bus Station.

Another of the forty-four-strong batch introduced in 2011 is shown here. DN33643 (SN11 BPY) is seen here having just left Lea Interchange garage, out of service. The garage is located near to the Olympic Park in Stratford. Taken in July 2012, during the London 2012 Olympic Games, this photograph provides a brief snapshot of the variety of vehicles that were used on Olympic shuttle duties.

Twelve Enviro400s were taken into stock during the summer of 2012 and entered service at the end of September on route 23. Representing the batch here is DN33778 (SN12 AVU) seen waiting at traffic lights before crossing Trafalgar Square, bound for Liverpool Street Station. They displaced a similar number of Wright Eclipse Geminis from this service.

Twenty-two Hybrid Enviro400s were taken into stock by First London, during April and May 2012, to convert route 23 to the type. DNH39112 (SN12 APZ) is seen passing the Theatre Royal, Haymarket. Allocated to Westbourne Park Garage, these vehicles transferred to Tower Transit in June 2013. (David Beddall)

Seen running with its new operator is DNH39115 (SN12 ARU). It is seen heading towards Westbourne Park travelling through Aldwych. November 2018 saw the restructure of some routes in central London. Route 10 was withdrawn, being replaced by various other routes, one of which was the 23. The Marble Arch to Aldwych section of the 23 was withdrawn, with it being re-routed from Marble Arch to Hammersmith Bus Station.

The West London location of Ladbroke Grove, close to the Westbourne Park terminus, sees route 23 passing both ways. It is at this location we find Tower Transit's DNH39123 (SN12 ATF) working a journey to Aldwych. The 23 was withdrawn between Aldwych and Liverpool Street at the end of September 2017 before the re-routing mentioned above.

First London was successful in winning the tender for route 425 (Stratford–Clapton) from Go-Ahead London. The first of the batch, DN33789 (SN13 CGY), is seen here at Stratford Bus Station. The route was extended to serve Ilford in December 2018.

Arriva The Shires took stock of a solitary Enviro400 in February 2008, entering service in March. It was ordered against the TfL school contract on route 642. It was, however, used on any of the TfL services operated from the company's Garston garage. It is seen here on route 258 (Watford Junction–South Harrow Station) passing Harrow Bus Station. Originally numbered 5448, SN08 AAE passed to Arriva London along with Garston in 2016 when it was renumbered T199.

Arriva London was late in taking examples of the Enviro400 into stock. It was not until 2008 when the first examples entered the fleet. The initial order for fifty E400s was soon increased to sixty-five, these were to cover routes 102, 135 and 466. T2 (LJ08 CVT) was originally operated on route 102 between Edmonton Green and Brent Cross. Allocated to Palmers Green garage, the 102 batch could be found on other double-deck routes from this garage. This is the case here where it is seen operating route 329 at Turnpike Lane, having just left the terminus bound for Enfield. A comparison can be made here of the classic and MMC front styling.

Brent Cross Shopping Centre finds T4 (LJ08 CVV) and T37 (LJ08 CUG) on layover on their intended route 102. An example of the ALX400 can be glimpsed on the left of the photograph. The basic Arriva London livery can be clearly seen in this view. (David Beddall)

Arriva London took stock of their first Enviro400s during 2008. Sixty-five were ordered against routes 102, 135 and 466. T14 (LJ08 CVG) was one of the first examples to be delivered in April 2008 to Barking garage. It originally operated on route 135 but is seen here at East Croydon after transfer to Croydon following the loss of the 135 to Go-Ahead London in 2015.

2008 saw the introduction of route 135 between Old Street Station and Crossharbour. A number of Enviro400s were taken into stock by Arriva London's Barking garage to operate the service. T14 (LJ08 CYK) is seen loading at Crossharbour.

2009 saw the start of a programme to withdraw the Mercedes-Benz Citaro articulated buses from London service. One such route to lose these vehicles was the 38 (Victoria–Clapton Pond). Seventy double-deckers were ordered to replace the bendy buses. The bulk of the order comprised fifty-seven Wright Gemini 2 DLs, with the gap being filled by eighteen Enviro400s. Representing this batch is T69 (LJ59 ADV), which arrived at Clapton garage in September 2009. It is seen on Mare Street, Hackney, passing the entrance to its home garage. The small batch later went on to convert route 78 to the type. (David Beddall)

T74 (LJ59 ABK) was another example delivered in September 2009 to Clapton garage. It is seen here at Hampstead Heath before heading back south of the river to Tesco on Old Kent Road.

Arriva London was successful in winning route 133 from London General in September 2009, when an order for thirty-four Enviro400s was placed. The route and vehicles were allocated to Norwood garage. T112 (LJ59 LYP) is seen passing through Streatham Hill sporting a Vodafone all-over advertisement.

Arriva London South took stock of twenty-seven Enviro400s during the summer of 2010 at Croydon and Thornton Heath garages. T118–121 were allocated to the former garage, whilst T122–144 were allocated to Thornton Heath, where they were predominantly used on route 250. However, the batch also strayed onto the 109 and 198 as needed. T142 (LJ10 HTU) is seen on the forecourt of its home garage displaying route 198 on its blinds.

An impressive ninety-three Enviro400s were taken into stock by Arriva London in 2010. Originally allocated to Lea Valley garage for route 341, T158 (LJ60 AVF) arrived in September, 2010. It later transferred south to Croydon where it topped up the native examples. It is seen here nearing East Croydon Station.

From 24 April 2017, routes serving the Barkingside area of North East London gained route branding and coloured route numbers as a six-month experiment to encourage more people to use buses in the area. T169 (LJ60 AUU) is seen here carrying route branding for route 150 (Chigwell Row–Becontree Heath), passing through Ilford Broadway.

T181 (LJ60 AUK) was originally allocated to Barking garage for use on route 150, arriving in September 2010. It is captured in this view passing Walthamstow Central Station on a rail replacement service in March 2019. By this point it was given new Arriva logos.

April 2011 saw an order placed for a further seventy-eight Enviro400s for the North London routes 144, 279 and W3. Delivery was completed between January and February 2012. Lea Valley-based route W3 was allocated twenty-three examples (T201–223). T214 (LJ61 CGO) is seen here crossing the top end of Wood Green town centre bound for Finsbury Park Station.

The longest route of the three to receive the 2012 deliveries was the 279 (Manor House–Waltham Cross). T224–259 were allocated to this route, operating from Ponders End garage. T254 (LJ61 LKC) is seen here departing Waltham Cross Bus Station for its journey to Manor House. Waltham Cross itself is on the edge of the TfL operating area.

For completeness, the 144 (Muswell Hill–Edmonton Green) gained the last nineteen (T260–278) of the 2012 deliveries. Representing the batch here is T268 (LJ61 LJU), seen on layover at Muswell Hill. The restyled bumper, distinguishing the newer E40D model, can be seen here. (David Beddall)

2013 saw the arrival of nine Enviro400s (T279–287), ordered against the renewal of the contract for route 60. However, like other Enviro400s based at Croydon, they formed part of a common user pool of vehicles. This is illustrated above as T281 (LJ13 CHO) negotiates Tooting Broadway, starting its journey on route 264 for Croydon town centre.

Arriva Kent Thameside won the contract for route 229 from London Central in 2015. For this, and the retention of route 492, thirty-one Enviro400s were ordered and were intended to have been numbered 6485 to 6515 by the company. From January 2016 the London operations came under control of the main Arriva London fleet, with the vehicles officially transferring across to this operator later in the year. As a result, the batch gained rolling stock numbers T301–331, all being allocated to Dartford. T307 (LK65 ENV) is seen about to enter Bexleyheath town centre bound for Thamesmead.

Fellow stable mate T310 (LK65 ENY) is seen here completing a journey on route 492, about to enter the bus station at the Bluewater Shopping Centre in Kent, closely followed by a Gillingham-based E400 MMC with Arriva Southern Counties. The shopping centre is again heavily served by bus routes, including a handful of TfL services.

Arriva London was re-awarded the contract for route 78 (Nunhead–Shoreditch) in 2015, for which they ordered nineteen Enviro400 City machines. Delivery of these vehicles was delayed with VLWs displaced from the 168 filling in for them in the meantime. The first seven arrived with Arriva during November 2015, with the full batch being in stock by January 2016. HA1 (LK65 BYX) is seen loading in Peckham town centre. The initial nineteen were allocated to Ash Grove garage.

Thirty-four further examples of the Enviro400 City were taken into stock by Arriva London during November and December 2016 to convert routes 133 and 333 to the type, the latter route being won from London General. HA29 (LK66 GZY) is seen crossing London Bridge, bound for Streatham Station. The City model took features from the New Bus for London, including the staircase and the destination display.

Both routes 133 and 333 serve Elephant & Castle. This is where we find HA49 (LK66 HBZ), nearing journey's end just off the main roundabout. The nearside styling can be seen clearly in this photograph.

ADH9 (SN60 BYD) is seen rounding the corner from Piccadilly Circus to Haymarket whilst heading for its stand just off Haymarket itself. The subtler hybrid branding applied to the newer hybrid vehicles can be seen at the rear of the vehicle. The ADH class were London United's first experience of operating the Enviro400. (David Beddall)

In June 2014 a handful of London Buses gained a part advert to promote the iBus technology installed on them. Showing off this livery is ADH12 (SN60 BYH), heading towards Acton Green, passing through Marble Arch. The ADH class were used to promote a number of different products.

London United retained the tenders for routes 81, 120 and 222 in 2011. For this the company ordered forty-five Enviro400s for delivery the following summer. The company gave the vehicles the ADE class code and allocated them all to Hounslow garage. ADE1 (YX12 FNG) is seen at rest in the new Slough Bus Station before travelling back to Hounslow.

ADE14 (YX12 FNV) is seen at the other end of the route parked at Hounslow Bus Station. The garage building can be seen in the background. The restyled front end can again be seen clearly in this photograph.

Seen out of its normal area of operation is London United's ADE45 (YX62 BZS). It is seen whilst on loan to sister company Quality Line (Epsom Buses), approaching Kingston's Cromwell Road Bus Station. It was loaned between October 2016 and May 2017 to cover for native DD15, which suffered accident damage.

20 October 2012 saw the introduction of the Enviro400 to London United's route 220 (Wandsworth–Harlesden). At this time the route transferred out of Shepherds Bush garage to Park Royal. ADE60 (YX62 BKO) is seen passing through Harlesden bound for Wandsworth.

Route 27 (Chiswick Business Park–Turnham Green) gained a fleet of twenty-nine Hybrid Enviro400s between January and March 2013, all being allocated to Stamford Brook garage. The first of the batch, ADH23 (YX62 FAU), is seen at Notting Hill Gate. (David Beddall)

ADL has a facility in Harlow, just north of London. This is where we find London United's ADH27 (YX62 FFB) and Arriva London's T256 (LJ61 LKE). Other than the black casing around the headlights, there is no difference in appearance between the standard diesel and hybrid Enviro400s. The engine of a Hybrid can be viewed on the Stagecoach Oxford example to the left of ADH27.

Hammersmith sees route 27 pass through in both directions. ADH29 (YX62 FHA) is seen exiting Hammersmith Bus Station carrying its new five-digit fleet number (ADH45029) applied to the RATP London fleet in March 2016.

Transport for London have run a couple of advertising campaigns to promote how many 'green' buses are operated in the capital. ADH45039 (YX62 FNZ) was used in 2018 to promote the 3,000 green vehicles that were operating in the capital. It is seen heading towards Chalk Farm at Notting Hill Gate.

ADH51 (YX62 FUU) is the last of the fifty-one hybrid Enviro400s to operate with London United. The impressive structure that is Baker Street Station can be seen in the background.

Harrow-based route H12 gained two sets of new buses in the autumn of 2018. Originally, a small batch of Wright Eclipse Gemini 3s took up service on the route prior to the intended batch of Enviro400 MMCs taking up service. ADH45279 (YX68 UNJ) is one such example seen passing through a wet Pinner town centre.

A similar batch followed in October for the take up of Harrow local service H14. ADH45294 (YX68 UOO) represents this batch, captured loading in Harrow town centre. The small RATP fleet names applied to these vehicles can be seen just behind the driver's window.

Thirteen Enviro400s were ordered by the Arriva Kent Thameside operation to restock route 160 (Catford Bridge–Sidcup), replacing older Alexander ALX400 bodied DAF DB250s. 6462 (GN61 JRO) was delivered to the company in December 2011, the batch being allocated to Dartford garage. It is seen near journey's end in Catford.

CT Plus purchased a solitary Enviro E40H on behalf of University College London, who would use the bus for research purposes. HEA1 (SN62 DND) arrived in December 2012 and entered service the following February on route 388. It worked the route alongside older East Lancs Myllennium bodied Dennis Tridents acquired nine years earlier. It is seen here heading for Blackfriars travelling down Bishops Gate close to Liverpool Street Station.

2015 saw CT Plus win the contract for route 26 (Waterloo–Hackney Wick) from Tower Transit. For this, the company ordered twenty-one Enviro400 City double-decks. Delivery of these vehicles took place in June 2016, with the contract starting in February 2016. To fill the gap until they had arrived, the company hired examples of the classic Enviro400 from Tower Transit. 2509 (SN16 OHY) represents the initial batch of Enviro400 Citys to be delivered to the company. It is seen leaving Waterloo for Hackney Wick.

Sixteen further examples arrived with CT plus for the renewal of route 388, which had been extended to Elephant & Castle from its Blackfriars terminus. It became common place for the 26 and 388 batches to appear on each of the routes. This is depicted here by 2526 (SN66 WRL), which is seen about to enter the Aldwych having just crossed Waterloo Bridge.

2528 (SN66 WRP) is seen passing through Bishopsgate, en route for Elephant & Castle on its intended route 388. The small fleet names applied to the batch can be seen in this photograph. A former ADL demonstrator was added to the fleet in February 2017 to make up numbers.

CT Plus took nine further examples of the Enviro400 City hybrids for the take up of route 20 (Walthamstow Central–Debden) from Go-Ahead London. 2546 (YX19 ORY) is seen departing Walthamstow Bus Station on its journey into Essex on its first day in service. The expansion of the CT Plus operation over the 2017–19 period led to a new garage being opened in the Walthamstow area, coded AW by the company as can be seen below the drivers cab in this view.

Ten former Abellio London Enviro400s passed to Ensign Bus during August 2016, before being acquired by tour operator Big Bus Company. LJ09 OKU, former Abellio 9485, was allotted rolling stock number DA230 in the Big Bus fleet. The new operator's livery suits these vehicles rather well. DA230 is seen rounding Hyde Park Corner.

South Mimms-based Sullivan Buses operates numerous school contracts around North London as well as being a common sight on rail replacement services across the capital. LJ09 OKB, former Abellio London 9469, is seen about to cross Putney Bridge on such duties. This was one of the batch returned off lease in August 2016 and sold via Ensign Bus. It passed to Sullivan Buses in November 2016 when it took up fleet number E40 with that company.

South Mimms-based Sullivan Buses won the contract for the 217 (Waltham Cross–Turnpike Lane) from Metroline, and commenced operation in June 2017. For this they took twelve Enviro400 MMCs into stock. E74 (JS17 SUL) is seen approaching the Turnpike Lane terminus, having already changed its blind for the return journey.

Not all Enviro 400s that operate into London operate on TfL routes. 2018 saw the transfer of Green Line service 702 (Windsor–London) from First Berkshire to Reading Buses. For this service, a number of Enviro 400s were drawn from their main fleet. Later, a number of buses in the fleet were trialled on the route to see which was best suited; the chosen vehicle was the Optare MetroDecker. 757 (YX64 VRT) is seen bound for Victoria, passing Hammersmith Bus Station. The vehicle was decorated in a special livery to mark the royal wedding in May 2018.

London Travel In also operate a couple of contract routes into London Victoria. Enviro 400 MMC SN18 KLP shows off the basic livery used by the company. It is seen rounding Marble Arch.